LOLA TUNG

EMERGING ACTRESS AND MODEL

BY MADDIE SPALDING

Core Library

An Imprint of Abdo Publishing
abdobooks.com

Cover image: Lola Tung attended the Chanel Tribeca Festival Artists dinner in June 2023.

abdobooks.com

Printed in the United States of America, North Mankato, Minnesota.
102024
012025

Cover Photo: Nina Westervelt/Variety/Getty Images
Interior Photos: Craig Barritt/Getty Images Entertainment/Getty Images, 4–5; Dominik Bindl/Getty Images Entertainment/Getty Images, 8, 40, 43; John Nacion/Getty Images Entertainment/Getty Images, 12–13; Red Line Editorial, 15; Deb Cohn-Orbach/UCG/Universal Images Group/Getty Images, 16; Amazon Studios/Album/Newscom, 19, 45; Lexie Moreland/WWD/Getty Images, 22–23, 29; Jose Perez/Bauer-Griffin/GC Images/Getty Images, 26; Sean Zanni/Getty Images for Phenomenal Media/Getty Images Entertainment/Getty Images, 32–33; Shutterstock Images, 35 (top left, top right, bottom left), 35 (middle left), 35 (bottom right); RW/MediaPunch/IPx/AP Images, 36

Editor: Kari Cornell
Series Designer: Marley Richmond

Library of Congress Control Number: 2024938337

Publisher's Cataloging-in-Publication Data

Names: Spalding, Maddie, author.
Title: Lola Tung: emerging actress and model / by Maddie Spalding
Other title: emerging actress and model
Description: Minneapolis, Minnesota: ABDO Publishing, 2025 | Series: Newsmakers | Includes online resources and index.
Identifiers: ISBN 9781098295714 (lib. bdg.) | ISBN 9798384916710 (ebook)
Subjects: LCSH: Tung, Lola--Juvenile literature. | Actresses--Biography--Juvenile literature. | Television shows--Juvenile literature. | Singers--Biography--Juvenile literature. | Stage actors--Juvenile literature. | Models--Biography--Juvenile literature.
Classification: DDC 791.43028092--dc23

CONTENTS

PRETTY
prime video
THE SUMM
NED
PRETTY
prime video
THE SUMM
I TURNED
PRE

4

A DEFINING ROLE

Lola Tung was in shock. She could not believe what she had just heard. She was on a Zoom call with author Jenny Han, some producers, and a director of the television show *The Summer I Turned Pretty*. The show was in development. It would be based on Han's book trilogy of the same name. The team was leading the casting process, and Tung had auditioned for the role of Isabel "Belly" Conklin. Belly was

Lola Tung attended the premiere party for *The Summer I Turned Pretty* in June 2022.

the main character. Han had just told Tung that she had landed the role.

This was a breakthrough moment in Tung's acting career. The 18-year-old was in her second semester of school at Carnegie Mellon University in Pittsburgh, Pennsylvania. She was studying acting, and she had performed in many school plays in high school. But this would be her first professional role as an actor.

THE AUDITION PROCESS

Tung sent in her audition video for the role of Belly in early 2021. This was during the COVID-19 pandemic, which affected the audition process. Tung had filmed her audition in her apartment with help from her roommates. A few days after submitting her audition, Tung heard back from the casting team. She was elated to learn that they wanted her to continue on in the audition process.

Over the next month, Tung completed several audition callbacks over Zoom. Some of her callbacks involved chemistry reads with other actors. During a chemistry read, several actors read scenes from the script together. This allows producers to see how the actors interact with each other.

Tung's acting talent impressed Han and the rest of the team. They invited Tung to a follow-up Zoom chat. They told her the call was to learn more about her. But they were actually calling to offer her the role of Belly! Tung excitedly accepted the offer. After the call

Tung paused for a quick photo with *The Summer I Turned Pretty* author Jenny Han, *right*, at an event at the Strand Bookstore in New York City in June 2022.

ended, she phoned her mother. She cried tears of joy as she shared the news.

STEPPING INTO THE SPOTLIGHT

By late April 2021, the media had announced the actors cast in the main roles for *The Summer I Turned Pretty*. Filming for the show began in July 2021. Tung was able to finish her first year of college. Then she traveled to Wilmington, North Carolina, where the series was filmed. But in 2022, she decided to take a break from her studies to focus on filming. Tung recognized that this would be a defining role for her. Han's book, *The Summer I Turned Pretty*, was a bestseller. Tung worked hard and dedicated herself to the role.

The Summer I Turned Pretty is about the changes that

happen in young adulthood. It explores themes of love and loss. Tung connected with these themes, and she saw parts of herself in Belly. Tung was only a few years older than the main character, who turns 16 early in the show. She could relate to Belly's exploration of her identity and relationships. Tung considered it an honor to play this character. It was important for her to portray Belly accurately and in a way that reflected Han's vision.

The series aired in 2022. It became an immediate hit. It ran for three seasons and gained widespread recognition for Tung. Tung had not expected this abrupt rise to fame. However, she enthusiastically accepted the challenge. Like the character Belly, Tung strives to stay true to her values and herself. As both an emerging actress and a model, she seeks out roles and projects that are meaningful to her.

STRAIGHT TO THE
SOURCE

Tung enjoyed playing Belly in *The Summer I Turned Pretty*. The character has many traits Tung related to and admired. Tung explained how she connected with the character in an interview with the *New York Times*:

> *I definitely think we're pretty similar, and I absolutely bring some of myself to her. It's only natural if you're playing a character, especially one so close in age. She's a very emotional person and leads with her heart and cares a lot about the people in her life, especially her family, even if it's hard to express that sometimes. I think she's bolder than I am, and she's more of a risk taker, and that was something I thought would be a challenge. But I really enjoyed getting to tap into that part of her, and I learned from her in that way. I stole some of her boldness.*

> Source: Christopher Kuo. "'The Summer I Turned Pretty': Lola Tung on Growing Up alongside Belly." *New York Times*, 13 July 2023, nytimes.com. Accessed 28 Jan. 2024.

WHAT'S THE BIG IDEA?

Read this part of Tung's interview carefully. What is the point that Tung is making? Which details support the main idea? Name two or three details that support this main point.

EARLY LIFE AND EDUCATION

Lola Tung's interest in acting began at a young age. Lola was born in New York City on October 28, 2002. As she was growing up in the city, she was influenced by the Broadway theater scene. Broadway is a street in New York City along which many theaters were built. *Broadway* is used to describe theater shows. Broadway shows are well-known around the world, and many actors move to New York City with the goal of acting in a Broadway show. Lola herself

Tung has been interested in acting and theater since she was a young girl.

was inspired by Broadway shows such as the musical *Hamilton*, which she saw with her mother and sister when she was in eighth grade. Throughout Lola's childhood, her family encouraged her exploration of acting. Lola's father was a musician, and her mother was an actor. They knew what it took to succeed in the creative arts. They supported Lola as she worked toward her dream of becoming an actor.

Lola's first acting experience happened when she was in the sixth grade. She auditioned for her school's production of *The Wizard of Oz* and got the part of the Tin Man. Lola was a shy child, but she soon discovered that she enjoyed being onstage. She also enjoyed the process that went into making a production, including the rehearsals, costumes, and makeup. Lola knew that she wanted to continue acting.

A FOCUS ON ACTING

After Lola completed middle school, her parents helped her enroll in Fiorello H. LaGuardia High School.

ACTOR DEMOGRAPHICS IN THE
UNITED STATES

These graphs show the racial and ethnic demographics of actors in 2011 and 2021. What do you notice about how these demographics have changed in ten years?

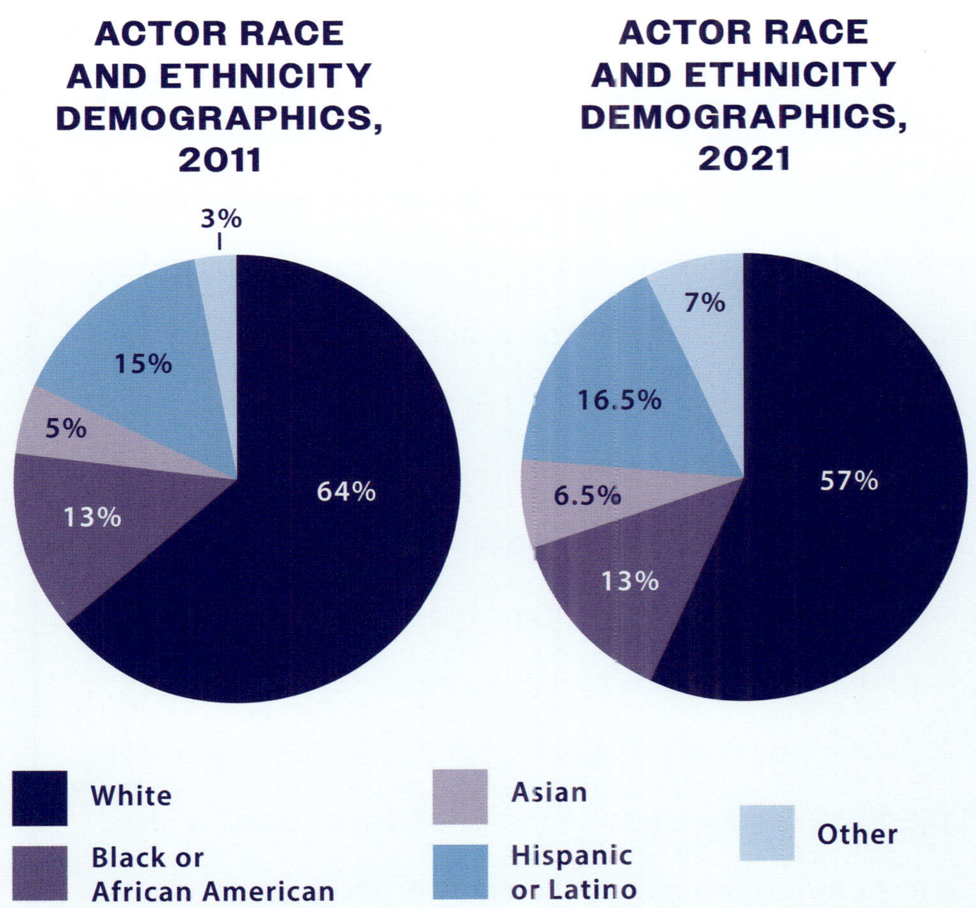

At LaGuardia High School, Tung appeared in productions on the same stage where actors such as Timothée Chalamet and Jennifer Aniston had performed years earlier.

LaGuardia is a well-known performing arts high school in New York City. As she took acting classes at the school, Lola became more serious about pursuing an acting career. She joined an outside theater group as well.

Lola's acting experience in high school ended with a senior showcase project. She knew this project could help launch her acting career. Each year, talent managers watch LaGuardia senior showcase projects for students they want to sign for professional acting roles. Lola submitted a video monologue for the showcase. She recorded it from her bedroom. After graduating she decided to further her education at another prestigious acting school. She had been accepted into the drama program at Carnegie Mellon University. She was eager to take this next step in her acting journey.

FROM STAGE TO SCREEN

In the fall of 2020, Tung moved to Pittsburgh for her first semester at Carnegie Mellon. She lived with roommates in an apartment in the city. Her roommates were also drama majors at Carnegie. Tung became close with them, and they supported each other in their acting pursuits.

Due to the COVID-19 pandemic, Tung had been unable to visit the college's campus for a tour before moving. However, she soon discovered that she enjoyed Pittsburgh and her college acting classes. She felt a sense of belonging and enjoyed being around people who shared her same passion for acting.

Although Tung dreamed of an acting career after college, she was focused on her studies at Carnegie.

She did not expect the exciting news she received while in her second semester of school. Carissa Stewart, a talent manager who had seen Tung's senior showcase video, reached out to Tung. Stewart was impressed by Tung's acting talent. She offered to be Tung's manager, and Tung accepted. Then Stewart shared that she had an upcoming audition in mind that she encouraged Tung to pursue. Stewart thought Tung would be

Tung and Christopher Briney shared a scene on the set of *The Summer I Turned Pretty* in 2022.

perfect for the role of Belly in the Amazon Prime show *The Summer I Turned Pretty*. This was Tung's first acting audition, and it became her first professional acting role.

SUCCESS AND SELF-DISCOVERY

For Tung, the next few years of filming were a life-changing experience. Amazon Prime renewed *The Summer I Turned Pretty* for a second season before the first season had even premiered. The studio recognized that given Han's fan base, there was a large audience for the show. As predicted, the show was instantly popular. Tung went from being a largely unknown actor to a household name. The show's first season was filmed during the summer of 2021. The second season, which was filmed the following summer, was even more of a hit than the first. The show's viewership more than doubled.

Tung believes that adjusting to fame would have been difficult without her strong support system. She developed close friendships with her costars as well as author and show creator Jenny Han. Tung was able to manage stress with the help of her fellow actors, her family, her friends, and Han.

In the series, Belly also develops strong relationships while learning more about herself. Tung believes that she grew alongside Belly in these ways too. Tung viewed this acting experience as a journey of self-discovery. The success of *The Summer I Turned Pretty* gave Tung the confidence to explore her other creative passions and continue growing her career.

EXPLORE ONLINE

Chapter Two explores Tung's journey to becoming a professional actor. The website below shares Tung's biography and interests. How is the information from the website the same as the information in Chapter Two? What new information did you learn from the website?

LOLA TUNG

abdocorelibrary.com/lola-tung

MODELING AND ACTIVISM

With the success of *The Summer I Turned Pretty*, Tung gained a large following. The show appealed to a wide audience, and Tung had millions of supporters who were interested in whatever creative projects she pursued next. And like many actors, Tung had other interests outside acting. Among these interests was a passion for fashion.

Tung had been drawn to fashion since childhood. She was inspired by New York

Tung, who has long been a fan of the fashion industry, attended the Bach Mai Ready-to-Wear Runway Show in September 2023.

City's fashion industry. Many fashion designers and manufacturers live and work in the city. Tung saw how clothing could be another avenue in which she could express herself. So when the clothing brand American Eagle approached Tung and her *The Summer I Turned Pretty* costars with an offer to model a new clothing line, Tung excitedly accepted. She knew of this brand, and its clothing reflected her own personal style.

American Eagle's new clothing line,

called The Summer of Us, was released in May 2023.
It was inspired by the fashion of the characters in *The Summer I Turned Pretty*. It featured summer- and beach-themed clothing. The Summer of Us line promotes the idea of connection, breaking down the feelings of loneliness many people experienced during the COVID-19 pandemic. Developing connections and friendships is an important theme in the show.

USING HER VOICE

For Tung, fashion has also served purposes beyond self-expression. She saw the potential to use fashion as a form of activism. Her parents had always encouraged Tung to speak up about causes that were important to her. Tung did this on social media, but she also used modeling as a way to raise awareness of issues.

One issue that is important to Tung is climate change. Climate change describes the shifts in weather patterns around the world that have been happening since the mid-1800s. Scientists have observed a rise in

Tung stands up for causes she believes in. On August 2, 2023, Lola Tung, *left*, walked the picket line with Minnie Mills, *right*, in New York City in support of the Screen Actors Guild.

Earth's average surface temperature. This phenomenon is called global warming. It has led to an increase in extreme weather events such as flooding and wildfires. Researchers have found that human activity contributes

to climate change.
Many industries that
produce goods,
including the fashion
industry, have a
negative impact on the
climate. Manufacturing
clothes requires the
use of natural resources
and factories. For
example, some fabrics
are made using wood
pulp. Workers have to
cut down a lot of trees
to harvest this pulp.
Harmful chemicals and
dyes that are used
to color clothing can
end up in rivers and
other water sources.

OTHER AREAS OF ACTIVISM

In addition to environmental issues, many other causes are important to Tung. These include women's rights, gun control, and animal rights. When Tung was 11 years old, she participated in a volunteer program that involved finding homes for dogs in shelters. This after-school program, called Unleashed, was offered to middle school–aged girls. Participants developed leadership skills while learning about animal rights issues. The girls played with dogs to get a sense of their personalities, which helped in finding homes for the dogs. This program helped Tung develop the confidence to speak up about causes that were important to her.

Also, discarded clothing that goes to landfills can contribute to pollution. In these ways, the fashion industry can have a negative impact on the environment.

Tung recognized how the fashion industry contributes to climate change. However, she also saw some companies that were making efforts to reduce their environmental impact. In the spring of 2023, Coach had this mission. Coach is a company that sells handbags, shoes, and accessories. A team of people at the company was working on a new brand called Coachtopia. The team invited Tung to help them launch this brand. The fashion items in this brand would be made only from recyclable and renewable materials. Tung models the brand's products.

Tung has also used her platform to raise awareness of overconsumption in the fashion industry. This happens when fashion brands mass-produce clothing

Tung attended a dinner to mark the launch of Coach's eco-friendly Coachtopia brand in April 2023.

and people buy more clothing than they end up using. Brands usually produce more clothing than they sell because mass production is cheaper than production on demand. Also, fashion trends change often, which can encourage people to buy more clothing than they need. This generates a lot of clothing waste. One solution to these problems is thrifting. Thrifting involves buying secondhand clothing. In this way, clothing that has already been worn can be recycled and not go to waste. Tung buys thrifted clothing and promotes thrifting to her followers.

As her audience and popularity grew, Tung considered it her responsibility to speak out about meaningful causes. She continues to do so as both an actor and a fashion icon. She uses her voice to help people understand societal issues and to promote change.

STRAIGHT TO THE
SOURCE

Tung embraces her role as an activist. She is always looking for projects that align with her values and promote a larger cause. In an interview with *FAULT Magazine*, she shared the personal values that are most important to her:

I believe there is always something to learn, regardless of age or experience. One thing I strive for is to be kind. Leading with kindness is important to me. . . . I believe we need to lead with love and prioritize caring for the planet and our people. It's something I'm grateful to have been raised with. Activism can be intimidating, and participating in protests or advocating for change may seem challenging, but not taking action is even more problematic. We need to be active in order to make a positive impact on society.

Source: Jacquex Frankel. "Lola Tung FAULT Magazine Covershoot and Interview." *FAULT Magazine*, 18 Aug. 2023, fault-magazine.com. Accessed 3 Mar. 2024.

CONSIDER YOUR AUDIENCE

Adapt this passage for a different audience, such as your friends. Write a blog post conveying this same information for the new audience. How does your post differ from the original text and why?

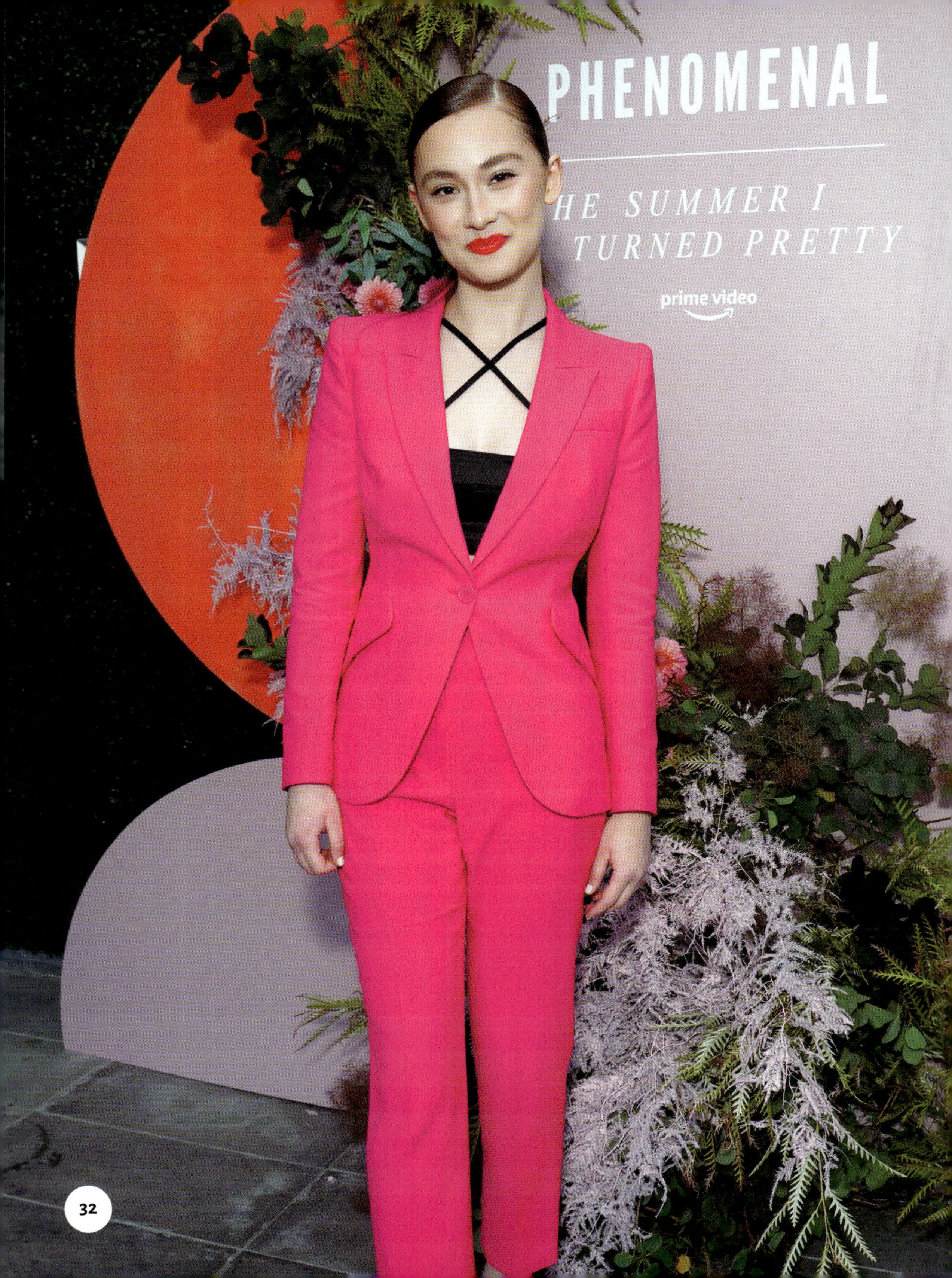

PHENOMENAL
HE SUMMER I
TURNED PRETTY
prime video

LOOKING TO THE FUTURE

While Tung has already had considerable success as an actor, she hopes that this is just the start of a long career in the creative arts. She continues to seek out projects that she is passionate about. She particularly enjoys work that involves acting or singing.

Tung initially shared her singing talents with the world through social media. Throughout 2021 and 2022, she recorded herself singing covers of well-known songs and

Tung's leading role in *The Summer I Turned Pretty* provided a successful launch to her acting career.

uploaded these videos to YouTube. A duet she sang with fellow LaGuardia classmate Aaron Syi in April 2021 became one of the most-watched Lola Tung videos. It generated more than 205,000 views. Tung and Syi sang the song "What Are We Waiting For." Viewers were impressed by both singers' talents and harmonization. As Tung's social media presence grew and *The Summer I Turned Pretty* became a hit show, her acting and singing talents became widely recognized. This opened the door to more opportunities.

TUNG'S BROADWAY DEBUT

Since childhood, Tung had dreamed of being a professional stage actor. Inspired by the New York City theater scene growing up, she aspired to one day perform in a Broadway show. So when she was cast in *Hadestown* in early 2024, it was a memorable moment for her. She landed the role of Eurydice (pronounced yer-IH-dih-see) in the Broadway musical. The musical is a retelling of the ancient Greek myth of Eurydice

BROADWAY BY THE NUMBERS

12.3 million tickets sold

4 shows attended by theatergoers on average

29% of audience members were people of color

65% of audience members were female

35% of audience members were from the New York City area

This chart shares information from a report on the demographics of Broadway theatergoers in the 2022–2023 season. Why do you think it might be important for shows to attract a diverse audience? How do these statistics reflect the popularity of Broadway shows? Does any of the information in this chart surprise you? Why or why not?

and Orpheus. These two characters fall in love, but tragedy interferes with their dream of living happily together. The villain Hades convinces Eurydice to work in his underground factory called Hadestown, which he promises will help her escape a life of poverty. Hades tricks Eurydice into signing a contract that says she

When Tung had the chance to play Eurydice in the Broadway musical _Hadestown_ at the Walter Kerr Theatre, it was like a dream come true.

belongs to Hades. However, Hades ultimately decides to let Orpheus lead Eurydice out of Hadestown as long as Orpheus does not look back at Eurydice while he is leading her. If Orpheus does this, Hades will keep Eurydice in Hadestown forever.

Tung was already familiar with the story of _Hadestown_. She had seen the musical with her father in early 2020. She was entranced by the music in the show.

It was an honor for her to step into this role and enter the world of *Hadestown* as an actor.

Tung played the role of Eurydice from February 9 through March 17, 2024. Two other actors had played this part before Tung. *Hadestown* originally debuted on Broadway in 2019. In that year, it won eight Tony Awards, including the award for Best Musical. The Tony Awards are annual awards given to Broadway plays and musicals. Tung was excited to be part of a show that was both

SUPPORT AND SELF-CARE

Performing in a main role on a Broadway show requires a lot of work. *Hadestown* is a popular musical, and there were eight shows a week when Tung took over the role of Eurydice. Live musical theater performance is different than acting for film or TV. Live performers do not have the option of redoing a scene. They try to hit every note and achieve peak performance at each show. Actors have to take good care of themselves to be able to do this. Tung's fellow actors in *Hadestown* were supportive of her, and they also modeled good self-care.

meaningful to her and critically acclaimed. Her fans were also excited to see her in this role.

When Tung stepped onto the stage for her first performance of *Hadestown* on February 9, 2024, the audience stood and applauded. They did the same at the end of the show. The performance showcased Tung's acting and singing talents and pushed her professionally. Eurydice is faced with tragic circumstances and experiences a range of emotions throughout the course of the show. Tung appreciated the challenge of playing such a complex character, and her depiction of Eurydice was praised by critics and fans alike. Tung's fan base grew as a result of this success. A video clip of Tung singing her solo "Wait for Me" from the musical received millions of views on TikTok. For Tung, this experience was a dream come true. Every time she stepped onto the Broadway stage, she felt as if she had stepped through a portal into a fantastical world.

BECOMING A PUBLIC FIGURE

Tung's many accomplishments have earned her widespread recognition as an actor, model, and singer. Starring in three seasons of *The Summer I Turned Pretty* was important to her, as this was Tung's breakout role, and she has since expanded her career into other areas. For example, Tung branched out into audiobook narration in 2022. She and her two costars narrated *The Summer I Turned Pretty* trilogy audiobooks.

On June 15, 2022, Tung, author Jenny Han, and host Lucy Feldman, *left to right*, discussed *The Summer I Turned Pretty* at New York's Strand Bookstore.

The audiobooks had previously been recorded, but Tung and her costars re-recorded them for fans of the show.

The process of becoming a public figure has been exciting and daunting for Tung at times. Fans may believe they fully know and understand a person when that person is in the public eye. Tung has felt pressure to live up to other people's expectations, but she does not allow that to limit her. She considers herself a generally positive person, and she is always on the lookout for opportunities to grow, both professionally and personally.

FURTHER EVIDENCE

Chapter Four talks about Tung's experience starring in a Broadway show. What was one of the main points of this chapter? What key evidence supports this point? The article below shares more information about the Broadway theater district. Find a quote from this website that supports the main point you identified.

BROADWAY

abdocorelibrary.com/lola-tung

IMPORTANT DATES

October 28, 2002

Lola Tung is born in New York City.

2020

Tung moves to Pittsburgh, Pennsylvania, in the fall to attend Carnegie Mellon University.

Early 2021

Tung begins auditioning for the lead role of Belly in the TV show *The Summer I Turned Pretty*.

April 2021

The media announces that Tung has been cast as Belly.

July 2021

Filming of the first season of *The Summer I Turned Pretty* begins.

2022

Tung narrates audiobook versions of *The Summer I Turned Pretty* trilogy as the character of Belly.

2023

In the spring, a new sustainable fashion brand called Coachtopia is launched. Tung partners with the brand and models its products. In May, American Eagle's new clothing line inspired by *The Summer I Turned Pretty* is released. Tung and her two costars are chosen to model the clothes.

February 9–March 17, 2024

Tung stars as Eurydice in the hit Broadway musical *Hadestown*.

Tell the Tale

Chapter One of this book describes Tung's experience landing her first professional acting role as Belly in the TV show *The Summer I Turned Pretty*. Imagine that you are on a video call with filmmakers and you have just received the news that you will be starring in a new show. Write 200 words about this experience. How would you feel about and react to this news?

Dig Deeper

After reading this book, what questions do you still have about Lola Tung? With an adult's help, find a few reliable sources that can help you answer your questions. Write a paragraph about what you learned.

Take a Stand

Tung believes it is her responsibility to use her platform to speak up about causes that are important to her. The causes she is most passionate about are environmental activism, women's rights, gun control, and animal rights. Today there

are many social media outlets that people can use to advocate for causes that are important to them. Do you think this form of activism is effective? Why or why not?

You Are There

Chapter Four covers Tung's breakthrough role on Broadway as Eurydice in *Hadestown*. Imagine that you were in the audience during one of these performances of *Hadestown*. Write a letter home telling your friends about your experience. Be sure to include plenty of details about your observations and impressions.

GLOSSARY

acclaimed
praised and celebrated by
the public

activism
any action that promotes
political or social change

callback
in acting, an invitation
to return for a
follow-up audition

demographics
the characteristics of
a population

headshot
a close-up portrait of an
actor that is shared with
casting directors

monologue
a long speech performed by
one actor

pandemic
a disease outbreak that
spreads across a wide area
and affects many people

phenomenon
an observable event or fact

platform
an arena or space where
people can share their ideas

renewable
able to be used and then
easily replaced

theme
a story's main subject
or topic

ONLINE RESOURCES

To learn more about Lola Tung, visit our free resource websites below.

Visit **abdocorelibrary.com** or scan this QR code for free Common Core resources for teachers and students, including vetted activities, multimedia, and booklinks, for deeper subject comprehension.

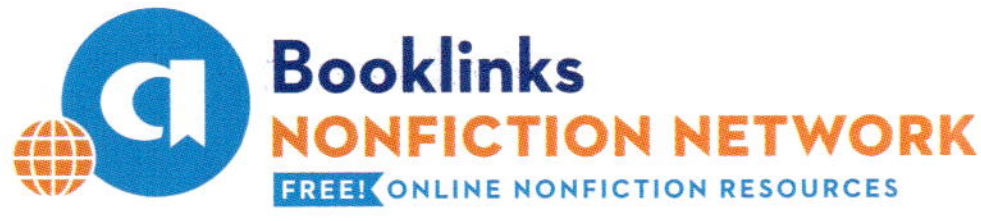

Visit **abdobooklinks.com** or scan this QR code for free additional online weblinks for further learning. These links are routinely monitored and updated to provide the most current information available.

LEARN MORE

Boone, Mary. *Hobbies If You Like Fashion*. BrightPoint, 2025.

Cornell, Kari. *Jobs If You Like the Creative Arts*. BrightPoint, 2025.

London, Martha. *Stopping Climate Change*. Abdo, 2021.

INDEX

About the Author

Maddie Spalding is a therapist and a writer. She lives and works in Minneapolis, Minnesota. She has written more than 50 children's books on a variety of topics.